To Paul, Ali... Sean Cheryl and of course Bailey?

Hope you like the book. It was a pain in the ass to write

Thomas P. Duyen

POINTERS

"Just a Few"

An Instructional Guide on Owning and Training
Medium and Large Breed Dogs

By
Thomas P. Dwyer

Copyright © 2003 by Thomas P. Dwyer

All rights reserved. No part of this book shall be reproduced or transmitted in any form or by any means, electronic, mechanical, magnetic, photographic including photocopying, recording or by any information storage and retrieval system, without prior written permission of the publisher. No patent liability is assumed with respect to the use of the information contained herein. Although every precaution has been taken in the preparation of this book, the publisher and author assume no responsibility for errors or omissions. Neither is any liability assumed for damages resulting from the use of the information contained herein.

ISBN 0-7414-1509-7

Published by:

519 West Lancaster Avenue
Haverford, PA 19041-1413
Info@buybooksontheweb.com
www.buybooksontheweb.com
Toll-free (877) BUY BOOK
Local Phone (610) 520-2500
Fax (610) 519-0261

Printed in the United States of America

Printed on Recycled Paper

Published June 2003

In Memory of

James E. Dwyer

Confirmation

Paul Pharmer

Hunting and Rearing

Table of Contents

Introduction 1
1 — Where to Start 4
  Training Difficulty 4
  Picking Your Dog 6
  Field Trials vs. Shows 6
  About Breeders 8
  The Neighbors 11
  Electronic Collars and Fences 12
  Dog Attacks 14
  Animal Control 14
2 — Looking for That Puppy 17
  A.K.C 17
  Money 18
  Pet Shops 20
  The Initial Visit 21
  What to Look For 22
  The Whistle Test 23
  Colors and Markings 24
  Umbilical Hernia 24
  Healthy Pups 24
  Puppy Handling 25
  Sire and Dam 25
  Whelping Box 26
  Extra Stuff 26
  Puppy Prices 28
  Co-Ownership 30
  The Lease 30
  Older Dogs 31
  Littermates vs. Brother and Sister 32
  Mixed Breed vs. Purebred 32
  Unregistered Purebred 33

3 — Bringing Your Puppy Home .. 43
Auto Confinement 43
Motion Sickness 44
Home at Last..44
Yellow Grass 46
Choosing a Veterinarian 47
Neutering & Spaying the Dog.............................49
Chocolate...50
Worms 51
Hair Loss & Fleas 52
Mange 52
Food, Collars, & Bedding 55
What to Feed Your Dog.......................................55
Lamb & Rice..56
Fat Dogs 57
Collars 57
Chewy Things..58
Bedding 59
Cedar...60

4 — Trainers............................... 62
Finding a Good Trainer.......................................63
Group Classes..64
Individual Classes 65
Individual Classes at Home.................................65
Kenneled Training 66
Specialty Classes...67
Fine Tuning...68
Doggie Boot Camp..68
So, You Want to Be a Trainer.............................69

5 — Domestic Training 72

Destruction by Puppies..73
The Piddle 74
Some Wasted Energy 76
Come When Called 77
Look Command 80
Kennel Training...80
Sit Command 82
Laying Down 83
Stay 85
Heeling...86
Heeling for Puppies...87
General Household Deportment 90
Dogs that Jump On You 94
Come When Called for Older Dogs 94
Whistle Training...97
Sit Command for Older Dogs 98
Laying Down for Older Dogs 99
Stay for Older Dogs 101
Heeling for Older Dogs.......................................102
So There You Have It 107

INTRODUCTION

A few years ago, a woman called me and asked if I would train her German Shorthaired Pointer named Jessie. It seemed that Jessie was having difficulty staying in the yard and the woman asked if there was anything I could do to correct this problem. The canine was also a little high strung and constantly paced both in and out of the house. She noted that the family loved the appearance of the dog but was nervous about Jessie's behavior. I reassured her that German Shorthairs do indeed make excellent house pets and that I would be happy to see what I might be able to do. "I must warn you," the woman concluded, "Jessie has trouble relating to men in general." I knew at once that I indeed, had a challenge.

Hunting dogs have similar characteristics; consequently children can play roughhouse with them without fear of bite or injury. There are some headstrong dogs, however, that make some breeds difficult to both live with and train. We all have images of dogs that hold fast in our minds. For example, the Brittany that you once owned as a child would have been relatively easy to train while the one that you own today might be almost unbreakable.

Most bold tempered hunting dogs come from field trial lines or from straight hunting stock and as such, they show a high degree of intelligence. They also possess the determination to do what they want. For example, if you were to place a roast in front of one of them and tell him or her not to touch it, they would be more than happy to accommodate your wishes. However, if you were to leave the room for ten minutes, you would probably return to find an empty dish.

The dogs who are more at ease with themselves are the ones who have been bred from *show* or *bench* stock. Although their faces reflect the same degree of intelligence, they seem better able to sit back and analyze a given situation. In spite of these differences, however, the difficulty in training both types remains essentially the same.

The woman had accurately described her dog. Jessie was a nice dog and well mannered but she clearly did not trust me nor did she wish to stand near me. While inside, she had the run of the house; outside, she was restricted to a 30 foot lead.

The first thing I had to do was educate the owner regarding the dog's disposition. All hunting dogs have energy to burn. Problems surface when they have no way to burn it. As a result, they often get into mischief that only hardens their existing temperament and leads to the development of bad habits. This would, of course, explain the dog's constant pacing. The challenge was to give Jessie an activity to look forward to. This would relax her, and in time, calm her down.

I spent the first three weeks simply getting near Jessie. At first she seemed light years away from a leash. Yet, within a short time, Jessie had learned to roam her yard without a lead and sit obediently with her owners on the back deck. To define her boundaries, I fitted Jessie with an electronic collar. She quickly came to know the space in which she would be permitted to maneuver. In a short while, her bad habits disappeared and, believe it or not, Jessie would eventually lie on the couch with me.

In this instance, there was nothing wrong with the dog or its owners. There was merely a lack of understanding about the characteristics of the breed from the time the pup was purchased until her early adulthood.

Although there are many excellent clinical books which can help dog owners through such difficult times, the reality is that trial and error as well as shared experiences are what usually gets passed along. This book is based upon such a premise and contains the benefit of experience that I believe will be most interesting and effective for both new and experienced dog owners alike. If there is a theme to this work, it is to *Tell it like it is*. I trust that is precisely what you will find passed along in the following pages.

Zeek
Photo by Jane Dwyer

CHAPTER I

WHERE TO START

If you're like the rest of us, once you bring a dog into your home, it will probably remain there for a very, long time. In light of this, the intensity of your search for that perfect dog should be right up there along side your other major lifetime acquisitions. Most people begin the process having a fair idea of precisely what type of dog they want but frequently get tired of looking and end up settling for an animal they perceive as *close enough*. Very often this is because the seller talks his way around the buyer's reservations. How many times have I heard the lament; "He looked so cute that I just had to take him home." Another of my personal favorites is, "I got him real cheap." Well, unfortunately *cute* works for only about three weeks -- then what? I'll discuss *cheap* at some length later on. For the moment, let's get back to the task of selecting the dog *you* want -- not the one that someone else thinks you should have. Here are a few other things you should consider before you actually start looking.

TRAINING DIFFICULTY:

     Given the benefit of years of experience, I give the pointing breeds the highest scores when rating dogs for their ability to accept training challenges. This would include the Weimaraners, Vizslas, English and French Pointers, German Shorthairs, Wirehaired Pointers, Griffons,

Pudelpointers, and Spinones. English and Gordon Setters rank a close second while Red and White Setters top the list of those being the most fun to train. Conversely, Irish Setters are the most difficult to work with.

Bringing up the middle would be the French Brittany and Brittany Spaniels. Don't let these little guys fool you. They are a compact wonder with a lot of orbs. Next comes the rest of the Spaniel family. You know them as Springers, Cockers, Field Spaniels, Clumbers and so on. Cocker Spaniels are by far, the easiest to train with one important reservation: most of the Cockers have fallen into the *money pit* inasmuch as their natural abilities have been bred out leaving them with badly diluted skills. This is also true for many other breeds that have been bred solely for commercial purpose. Remember that Dalmatian movie? Make sure that the line is strong.

Finally we come to the group known as Retrievers: Labradors, Chesapeake, Goldens, Flat and Curly Coated. They are, by any standard, among the easiest and most delightful dogs to train. Even the boldest retriever will readily adapt to the individual handler's method. Shepherds are a fine dog, although I rarely mention the breed in this manual, they are a stand up dog to train.

On the other hand, the hardest dogs that I have ever trained were the Hounds. From the Black and Tan Coonhound to the Beagle, these dogs were by far the strongest willed. If you are wondering about the terrier group; yes, I have owned a few and, with the exception of the Glenn of Imall Terrier and the Schnauzer, the less said the better. Although some of these breeds are not dealt with extensively in this book, most of what follows certainly can be applied to them.

PICKING YOUR DOG:

Now that you have sorted out what dog group you want, selecting your animal may not be as hard as it first seemed. All that remains is to narrow your focus within a particular breed. I remember the first dog that I wanted had to be a hunting dog that pointed (also known as a European Continental Hunting dog). I looked at the entire breed from the Vizsla to the Wirehaired Pointing Griffon and finally settled on the German Shorthaired Pointer. Besides being great for waterfowl as well as upland game, the Shorthairs temperament around children is superb. This combination of traits made it the best fit for both the field and around my home.

You are probably thinking that now is the time to run out and buy some books on pedigree. Hold that thought for a moment while you do two other preliminary things. First: talk to your family. Get them involved in the selection of the dog. What do they want most? Remember, they will also be sharing time and space with your new dog for many years to come so, their input is equally important. Second: talk to a breeder.

FIELD TRIALS VS. SHOWS:

Have you ever compared the physical characteristics of a hunting dog that was bred for field trials to another of the same breed who was bred to compete in the show ring? "That's a strange question," you say? If both dogs are the same breed and come from quality stock, how could they be physically different? Well, ironically, the science of breeding has always focused on complimenting dames and sires with matching characteristics to insure the extension of those traits in the litter. In the case of animals bred for show instead of field trials, those attributes are subtle but indeed different.

It is argued that show dogs are bred to the highest standards of their kennel organization and are entered into competition in order to determine which will be recognized as the "Best of Breed." Field dogs, on the other hand, are bred to perform herding or hunting tasks as efficiently as possible. They compete in trials or tests in order to determine which dog can accomplish that task best.

It is this distinction that is behind the fine-tuning which occurs within the different breeding groups. Although both types of dogs exist within the standards of the breed, they may well be physically different. For example, many field dogs are more muscular than their counterparts in the show arena. While this is desirable for the field dog, it is a definite liability for show. This also explains why there arc fewer dogs that are Dual Champions (winners of championships in both areas of competition).

I suspect that it is only a matter of time when many breeds will permanently subdivide (a case in point would be the Red and White Setter and Belgian Sheepdog) into separate breeding standards geared to their respective purposes. Although the purist might reasonably argue against this, I feel that professional breeding achieves its purpose only when it can produce dogs most suitable to the task at hand. In this case, we have two clearly different tasks.

While on this subject, I have often been corrected by my friends in the show world about my overuse of the term "bench show" when referring to a dog show. They are quick to remind me that there are no more shows in the United States where the dog is benched (lying or sitting on a crate or bench) until exhibited. Therefore they argue, the correct terminology is "dog show." This fails to explain the world famous Westminster Show where dogs are continuing to be benched before entering the ring.

ABOUT BREEDERS:

As in any profession, there are responsible breeders and bad breeders. Both are easy to find; just surf the web, or look in the yellow pages, journal advertisements, and the pet section of your local newspaper. When you contact a breeder, tell him that you are a first time buyer and ask him questions about his dogs. Are they good with children? Do they need a lot of room? Are they hyperactive? Most top-notch breeders will have little trouble fielding these questions -- chances are that you will find yourself engaged in a rather lengthily conversation concerning any or all of these traits. If and when this happens, you can be certain that you will have contacted one of the better breeders. Sometimes, you may even find a breeder who is more interested in seeing to it that you get the right animal even if it is *not* one he is selling. When this happens, you have found one of the *best*.

Tell the breeder that you are just browsing for the moment and ask to visit his facilities in order to look over his litter. This way, you will get to see some puppies first hand without making a commitment. The breeder may even be able to tell you where there are other litters to look at. It is also likely that he can inform you about trainers, vets, shots, or any of the many other things that you didn't even know enough to ask about. Remember that he knows his business and good judgement often dictates that you take advantage of it.

So, what happens if you run into one of those not-so-nice breeders that we also mentioned? In the first place, he will probably dismiss you when you ask for an informative visit. If on the off chance, he does invite you over, you will quickly recognize that he is not concerned about your animal education -- he only wants to sell you a dog. Ironically, this is an important part of the learning process and now you not only know who to stay away from but are also equipped to tell others why.

It is also good advice never to show an interest in the litter knowing that you are not going to make a purchase. The breeder (good or bad) will quickly discover such a deception. Chances are, not only will you be politely dismissed, but you may not be welcomed back. Be up front, and you will have acquired a valuable resource for the long haul. The good breeders can really help you if you are honest with them. Trust me!

I have also noticed the tendency of a few breeders to ignore the wants and needs of the buyer while they set aside the proper selling etiquette. These guys tend to cluster into self-serving groups and set themselves as the authoritative high priests before whom the uninformed public must genuflect. You will readily recognize them by their inflexible attitude and condescending manner. Unfortunately, these guys drive many an uninformed beginning buyer to the backyard breeder where he is just as likely to make an expensive and inappropriate purchase. Hopefully, this is a short-lived trend. For the most part, there are many courteous and knowledgeable breeders who will place your needs and the welfare of their animals on a much higher plane.

In any event, if and when you contact the right breeder and ask all of the right questions, it is entirely possible that you will still not be able to make a decision. This is the point at which many folks cave in and compromise with a dog that seems to be *good enough*. I cannot caution you enough to avoid this trap. You have done a great deal of homework up to this point but feel that you are running out of the time that you initially reserved for this project. When this happens, it's time to regroup and come up with a new schedule. You wouldn't buy a house or an automobile that was just *good enough*, so, why a dog? It may be time to slow down just a tad and do some more formal research.

Now go out and buy the pedigree book that you were thinking about earlier! Chances are, you will find a very good book on the particular dog that you were originally interested in. Many authors have done extensive research on their favorite breed and the results of their efforts may be found in any reliable bookstore or on the Internet. You will also find many fine resources in your local library as well as in the trade journals.

THE NEIGHBORS:

Having dealt with such heady matters, let's now think about things a little closer to home, your home. That nice Mrs. Jones (the one with the cats?) who lives down the street may be very sweet but add a dog to the neighborhood and you will likely see a dramatic social change in her behavior. How your new dog will fit into the neighborhood is a serious consideration; consequently, temperament and trainability become major elements of the selection process.

Living in the country makes adjusting fairly simple, but the more congested the neighborhood, the more trouble Spot will get into. Each situation is different. If you live in an area full of dogs, then do as the Romans do, but if you're the only house on the block with a dog then act responsibly and use appropriate methods to confine man's best friend. Your responsibility will also extend to noise control (also known as barking). There are various ways to control this, but if your dog is out of doors 24 hours a day then it may become necessary (especially in the case of an older dog) to consider using an electric anti-bark collar. This will quickly end all unwanted morning and evening concerts. If, by chance you live next door to the Noiseandclatter family and their kids drive snowmobiles and motorcycles all over the place at Godawful hours, you might be tempted to let your new pup handle the matter with a few noisy 3:00 AM solos. It would be a mistake, however, to put the animal into the middle of a personal problem. So, handle the matter using reasonable solutions. It also makes for a less confused dog.

Being a good neighbor also extends into the area of damage control -- in a literal sense. If Spot wanders off one morning in the spring and digs holes in that nice Mrs. Jones's yard, chews up her flowerbed, and trees all of her cats; don't go into denial. The dog's behavior is your responsibility. Fix the holes, replace the flowers, and get her cats back down in one piece. Who knows? You might become great friends.

ELECTRONIC COLLARS AND FENCES:

During domestic training exercises, I suggest the use of the electronic training collar. I do so with four important cautions:

1. The collar should be used only *after* the dog has been taught a specific command.
2. Only adults who have been properly trained in its operation should use a collar and children, of course, should never use one.
3. The collar should only be used to deter bad habits.
4. It should never be used as a form of punishment.

Having said that, collars come in all sizes and shapes. They range from the smaller, lower charged, anti bark collars to the larger, long range units which are capable of sending a signal over two miles. In order to find out which best suits your needs; talk to someone who already has one then discuss it with a trainer. Finally, contact the company who makes or sell them and ask for a catalogue.

Since the dog's safety is paramount, quality is the most important consideration when purchasing an electronic training collar. Less expensive models such as those used to control barking often tend to damage the skin, especially when worn for prolonged periods of time. Skin damage may also occur when using some of the better products, particularly if you have a problem dog who is hard to break. *Swat®,* a waterproof based fly repellent for wounds and sores, primarily on horses, will fix the sore handily.

Learning how to properly use a collar often takes as much patience as training the dog. There are some fine books that will enable you to sharpen your technique and many of them are available from the company that sold you the collar. Most reputable trainers will also be more than glad to demonstrate the do's and don'ts to you.

Around the yard, an electronic fence works just as well. In this case, the signal carrying wire is buried slightly below the surface of the ground and is used to mark the particular area that you wish to fence in (newer models are wireless). As in the case of the collar, quality varies with price. Stay away from the lower end of the price line because the less expensive wires will not withstand long term burial. Better yet, let a professional installer put it in for you. Most reputable dealers will come to your home, install the fence, and make sure that your dog becomes familiar with the perimeter markers that define where the wire is buried.

In communities where there are leash laws, a properly installed fence is particularly important. It's also a great training tool. Get the best one that you can afford, use it judiciously and, as with the training collar, check it periodically for wear and damage.

DOG ATTACKS:

At the risk of belaboring the obvious, I want to remind you that *all dogs bite* - without exception. A dog will bite for any of three reasons:

1. He is frightened, or feels that he must protect his property, or you.
2. He is in pain.
3. He was trained to bite.

In reality, there may be more than three reasons; nevertheless, these are the three issues that I am concerned about. Normally, none of the breeds we have been covering in this book would commit an unprovoked attack on one of your family members yet, if this should occur, then the dog must go. If it happens once, you can be reasonably sure that it will happen again and you must adjust to the fact that he is no longer part of the family. While this may seem somewhat heartless, there is no real room for compromise. Bear in mind, however, that dogs play with their mouths open so, get to know the difference between aggression and normal behavior.

ANIMAL CONTROL:

It's well worth the time and trouble to get to know your Animal Control authorities. I cannot overstress the importance of finding out ahead of time about such matters as local leash laws, quiet hours, and proper pooper scooping. The majority of problems that require Animal Control intervention usually involve a new puppy in new surroundings. How well he behaves may very well determine whether or not he stays.

Collars come in all sizes and shapes. They range from the smaller, lower charged, anti bark collars to the larger, long range units.

Millbrook's Tombe the Bombe
Photo by Diane Doering

S.R., Cedarbay's Mousse-Man Cometh, JH,WC Along with
Marianne L. Rousseau of Cedarbay Kennels
Photo by Kim Leeman

CHAPTER II

LOOKING FOR THAT PUPPY

Probably the best way to find a reputable breeder is simply to ask a few owners, trainers or veterinarians for their recommendation. Many good breeders also advertise in the pet section of your local newspaper so, that's as good a place as any to begin puppy shopping. If that doesn't work, expand your search to include the Internet, as well as out of town, statewide, and regional papers. Many breeders are also listed in dog magazines, but get your checkbook ready; they could prove to be expensive. There may also be local dog clubs and rescue leagues in your area that can help. Nationally, there is an excellent resource: kennel clubs.

A.K.C:

Most folks think of the American Kennel Club as merely a place to register their newest acquisition; consequently, they buy a dog, mail in some paperwork, and then forget that the organization exists. In point of fact, the AKC has a wealth of information. They have data on almost anything concerning purebred dogs that you would want to know. In addition, they can help you find breed clubs who will in turn, let you know about the availability of a new litter. All you have to do is contact them.

MONEY:

For some people, money is no object, while others must try to get the best deal they can afford. There is however, a third class of consumer out there who is just plain cheap.

Some time ago, my shorthair presented me with a litter of three. A gentleman from the city called and said he wanted to see them. When he arrived, he fell in love with one of the males and bubbled over with questions about breeding and bloodlines, which I was happy to answer. He said that for a *good dog*, he expected to pay a *good price*. He further explained how he expected to enroll in one of the areas finest clubs and have the puppy sent out to be trained. I was impressed and told him I would contact him as soon as the puppies were available. When I finally called him back, he advised me that he had reconsidered his position and that he would now take one of the pups off my hands for $150 less than I was asking. It seemed that Diamond Jim was willing to pay top dollar for everything but the dog itself. I soon sold the dog elsewhere.

The point to all of this is that when you are dealing with a quality breeder and he is offering you a quality dog for a fair market price, don't dicker. Chances are, there is someone else who recognizes quality and will buy the dog from right under your nose. The same is true for many of your major life purchases. Although you may be looking for blue ribbon qualities in a dog, remember that the breeder didn't get the dog for free. There were stud expenses, shots, food, shelter and an endless array of other costs associated with having and raising a litter. If you want to shave points on the price of a dog, go to one of those "bad" dealers that we mentioned earlier, pick out a puppy, get a price, wait about four weeks and see if that puppy is still there. Better yet, see if the price has dropped. If it has, offer him less. If he accepts, then you both got what you deserved.

Most quality show and field dogs will fetch top dollar while others equally as good, never make it into the ring because their breeders can't afford the competition expenses. In many other cases, they simply don't care about titles. In either event, there are some top quality dogs available for discriminating buyers who simply want the best.

On the other hand, there are breeders who are only trying to squeeze a dollar from a litter who's Dam never should have been bred in the first place. If you have done the homework; which we discussed in Chapter I, the breeder wouldn't be able to talk you into anything you did not want. If you really must have a bargain, then I would recommend going to a Rescue League and locate the dog you want. There are a lot of acceptable dogs that were taken in by people looking for bargains who eventually abandoned their animals.

Probably the safest play is to find that reputable breeder, select a pup, and leave a small deposit. When the puppies are ready, he will call you. If you no longer like what you see at this point; step away from the deal. Your deposit only gave you first choice on that particular dog and it will likely be returned because the breeder is confident that he will sell the dog elsewhere. Caution: only use this tactic during the first 6 weeks the pups are born. Otherwise, the deposit might be non-refundable.

PET SHOPS:

Most pet shops are a great place to pick up leashes, food, books, tidbits and fish. If you want to buy a puppy there, I would caution you to think again. I have always fancied that I could turn a quick buck by picking up some puppies and setting them out in a cardboard box on a busy street corner. I envision children passing by and tugging on their parents sleeve shouting, "Look Mommy -- aren't they cute?" The problem with this scenario is that like most reputable breeders, I care who I am selling the dog to and what happens to them in their new home.

Similarly, when folks pass that doggie in the pet shop window, they probably think what a cute pet he would make and want badly to take him home, where he will be so much better off. Well, that's part of the gimmick and sometimes it even comes with a pedigree. One of my friends purchased a Samoyed named Mica from a pet shop for those very reasons. He would later discover that Mica was ill from having previously eaten through sheet-rock. This was likely the result of being kenneled in small quarters for long periods of time and boredom always creates havoc.

When you are looking through those pet shop windows, pay attention to the space allocated to the animals. Some pet shops confine puppies in areas no larger than fish tanks. Consider if you will, the pheasant. If I wished to house pheasant for the purpose of training my dogs, I am required by my state to allow for a minimum of six square feet per bird and that is perfectly reasonable. I have, however, seen dogs three times the size of a pheasant stay in pet shops for up to six months with less space than that.

In fairness, some pet stores will go to great lengths to provide you with information about their puppies and from time to time some of them will even get their dogs from local breeders. Whatever the case, if you want to buy a dog and have confidence in what you are getting, it is always best to visit the puppy in its whelping box.

THE INITIAL VISIT:

Your first visit to a breeder can indeed, be an informative experience. For example, you will find them in all sorts of environments: in town, the suburbs, backyards, or wandering estates. Depending upon the whims of the breeder, you may find a half dozen Labradors wandering around the house or lounging in the front room. On the other hand, some keep their dogs outside 24 hours a day and only bring them in during extremely cold weather. Don't let this distract you. Pay close attention to the more important characteristics: behavior, general appearance, and disposition.

Although you may be anxious to see the puppies, you will likely be invited to relax and chat a while over a cup of coffee. This is a critical time for both you and the breeder. While you are sizing up the breeder, he will also be deciding whether or not he wants to sell you a dog. Sooner or later, you will find yourself in the puppy room or outside on the lawn playing with the little buggers. The breeder will be there with you and let you know if you do something wrong to one of the dogs. When you are done playing, you should have a lot of questions. You are looking for the right dog and he is looking for the right owner.

A friend of mine was looking for a companion dog. She set her sights on the Golden Retriever. A fellow worker in her office, who was also a breeder, told my friend that she was expecting two litters of Golden Retrievers. The breeder brought in photo albums filled with fine specimens. My friend was so pleased with the pictures that she made an appointment to see the litter. Upon her arrival, she found both dams to be in horrible condition. They were overweight and exhausted -- much too tired to deal with the puppies. If that weren't enough, the breeder was unable to certify the lineage of the parents. The deal soured on the spot. The key points to this story were not the number of litters but rather their quality and the lack of documented pedigree.

WHAT TO LOOK FOR:

The first thing to consider is the dog's disposition. You may observe this trait by watching the way that the new puppy socializes with his or her siblings. The dominant ones will stand out from the litter. You will recognize this by the exclusive definition of their tails. A pronounced tail signifies a sure-footed dog. Puppies also begin showing dominance even before they first open their eyes. They fight for the closest nipple; the best sleeping spots, (usually on top) and the right to pick play time. They might also be the first ones out of the whelping box. These actions are evidence of strong curiosity and courage.

Personally, I prefer curiosity combined with a moderately dominant personality. Again, this is recognized by a pronounced tail. Some would argue that a high level of dominance means that the dog will be a go-getter. This is a valid point; nevertheless, my experience suggests that the moderately dominant dogs will be just as successful because they are far easier to train. Most dominant dogs are usually the pick of the litter. Many breeders will tend to separate the dominant pup out early and sell him first, in the belief that it will enable those left in the litter to more readily develop. Conversely, others may use reverse logic by separating and selling the more timid dogs first.

If, on the other hand, you're in the market for a dog at the docile end of the scale, then look for the one that is less apt to join in on litter playtime. Again, the tail will be your barometer. While other pups will be yipping at something or someone, he will be the one who is most hungry and is the first to wake up yipping for food. Of course, he is always closest to dear old mom. I call these pups "Tie-Eye" and they are quite content just lying down beside you near the fire. They will also stay close to you in the field, if you find that desirable.

Last and certainly not least is the puppy that opened his eyes first and was weaned first. I have seen this combination of traits in many of my litters. This is usually an aggressive pup who's right in the middle of the roughhouse, having a grand time for himself. It's too bad that this type often gets overlooked. Those are the dogs that think.

THE WHISTLE TEST:

Another trick you can try is to whistle at the litter. Although all their heads will spring up, only one will be the first to come to you. The rest follow because of their pack instincts. Also watch for their tails to hook down, although some might not drop at all. Pay attention to them. At the same time, watch for any whom run toward you while looking at you. This is a good measurement of their ability to focus, and is an invaluable training characteristic.

COLORS AND MARKINGS:

All too often, the color and marking of the puppy are the determining factors in your decision making process. Where as cosmetic appearance is indeed important, it should not cloud your judgement when you weigh it in with all of the other traits that you are looking for. You may find that little birthmark irresistible but be certain that you are comfortable with all of the other markings and colors. The dog will retain his hue for a very long time.

UMBILICAL HERNIA:

Examine the animal's navel. If you find a bump roughly the size of your thumbnail, it is probably an umbilical hernia. This occurs when the Dam pulls the pup closer to her after birth in order to bite off the umbilical cord and clean the pup. It could be that she was whelping alone or that the breeder was simply busy with another pup. In either event, this defect should turn into a fatty ball and disappear. If it hasn't, ask the breeder if and when it was checked.

HEALTHY PUPS:

I realize that peeking at dog stools is not on your list of favorite things to do, but it is extremely important that it be on your checklist while visiting any litter. Watery stools might mean sickness. A distended abdomen could mean bloat. Tap the dog's tummy and see if it is taut as a drum. If it is, and it is not a blockage or bloat, it might be worms. Roundworm is very common in litters and has nothing to do with the quality of the pup. Slow mobility in any of the puppies could mean that they were recently wormed. If you find one who is slow, thin, or doesn't like to stand for very long; the whole litter could be sick. Start asking questions. Make sure that the breeder is taking care of the problem.

PUPPY HANDLING:

If you are fortunate enough to be permitted to handle any of the litter, remember; do not try to cradle them as you would a baby. Always grab them under the rib cage for support with their paws down. It is also important not to mess with Mother Nature. She gave them four legs for an important reason so, never try to make them dance on two legs. Their legs are still cartilage and although they are pliable, are vulnerable to damage. No matter, if you handle the pups incorrectly, the breeder will probably show you to the door.

SIRE AND DAM:

Always ask to see the Sire and the Dam. If they are not available, try for pictures or videotape. This will give you an excellent indication of what the pups will look like when they grow up. I don't usually pay much attention to the puppy's paws. They only indicate the bone structure of the puppy. Heads, however, are another matter. Chances are, if a pup has a big head, he will grow into a big dog. In the end the parents are the important things. If they complement one another, your puppy stands a good chance of inheriting their physical characteristics evenly.

WHELPING BOX:

Ask to see the whelping box. If it is clean with fresh newspapers, they were probably changed especially for your visit. Normally the box should have at least a couple of stools along with a trace of moisture. It is nearly impossible to maintain a clean box. If you find one, nobody is living there.

I once had a bitch that used newspapers for whelping only. Once completed, she pulled all of the newspapers out of the box so, all that remained was a bare wooden bottom on the box. I would spend hours on my knees cleaning it when the pups were weaning, but it always proved useless. I was forced to show the litter in the living room or outside. If someone asked, I would of course, show him the wretched old whelping box.

EXTRA STUFF:

After you have pretty much settled on the puppy that you want, have the breeder show you all of his paperwork. If it is permitted, leave the kids around to play with the puppies. While looking over the paper work, you might ask for an O.F.A. (Orthopedic Foundation for Animals) certificate. This will certify that both the sire and the dame are free from hip dysplasia (abnormal hip growth). The certificate will also show a graded measurement for dysplasia: excellent, good, fair, or poor. If dysplasia was found, some breeders will try to avoid the subject altogether. It might not even be part of the new buyer's selection criteria. In time, and with some experience, you may also be on the lookout for other things such as glaucoma, elbows, teeth, heart, and doggie v.d. The list will keep growing.

Ask also about the condition of the dam when she was whelping and how many litters she has produced. I use the general rule of thumb that no bitch should be bred under the age of two and then, only every two years for a maximum of three times, never past the age of eight. Overweight dogs also have a difficult time producing puppies. Too much strain is put on the bitch and it crowds the uterus. It stands to reason that a healthy bitch will deliver healthy pups.

Conversely, I knew some folks who had a 10 year old Shepherd who was slightly nearsighted and overweight. Somehow, she mated with a Springer and produced a litter. After the weaning was complete, the poor dog was very lame and almost blind. This seems practically criminal to me. The animal should have been spayed long ago.

There should also be a health certificate for each of the puppies in the litter. Ask to see it. It will certify that the puppies were wormed and had their shots. Also let the breeder talk about the litter. Encourage him to tell any little anecdotes or stories that he might remember concerning them. This might give you an idea of the character and temperament that the new puppy will be bringing into your home.

It is also wise at this time, to reach an agreement on any warranty that the breeder intends to attach to the sale of the puppy. Most reputable breeders will take the dog back if you decide after a short while, that you and the dog are not a good fit. It is also good to define the term "short while" and whether any refund will be full or partial. Breeders do not know what has happened to the dog, while staying with you. As far as he is concerned, the dog is to be returned and cared for. So remember, good breeders are just as concerned about the dog's welfare as you. This would be the case even if you had set the animal up a miniature Taj Mahal with a private Jacuzzi.

Throughout the process of negotiation, the breeder has been appraising you to determine that you are right for one of his dogs. The good ones will not sell a pup to someone until he thinks he knows something about that buyer. This is particularly true when he is backing up the deal with a strong warranty. There will be no sale if he suspects that the animal might be mistreated or neglected. So, if anyone is just trying to bring a dog home to test their children for allergies, they won't be getting one of his dogs.

PUPPY PRICES:

The price you pay for a puppy will vary according to the area where you buy him as well as the quality of the dog itself. For example, large dogs in the city might sell for less because of stiffer leash laws. There may also be a breeder near you who is flooding the market place and driving prices down. Pedigree is also a factor because dogs with papers will certainly bring higher prices than those without.

Generally speaking, the more expensive the dog, the better the care it will receive. I suspect that this is true because of more discernable buyers. That doesn't mean that the free pooch from the Animal League is likely to be mistreated. Rather, it simply suggests that folks often pay better attention to sizeable investments. Personally, I treat my two free dogs exactly the same as my top pedigrees. The unfortunate truth, however, is that dog pounds exist because many folks do otherwise.

Puppy prices can also vary within the litter itself. For instance, if females are in large demand in your area, males will become cheaper. Also, some litters contain what we call a *Runt*. This is the smallest of the lot and will usually bring less. Sometimes the price decreases as the litter gets older. On the other hand, when the breeder begins to train his older puppies, he can, and often will, increase the going rate.

I bought Dutchess, my first Shorthair, in 1979 for $125. This was a fairly modest price at the time. The litter was very well kept and in spite of marginal bloodlines, the puppies all showed good character. Dutchess was also the runt of the litter but I reasoned that I wasn't getting her for show or field trials; rather I wanted her for home and a little hunting. As it turned out Dutchess was the finest dog I have ever owned.

Lastly, if there is anything suspicious about either the dog or the breeder, walk away from the deal! Don't delude yourself that any potential problems will solve themselves down the road. If, on the other hand, you see a good match between you and the puppy, consider the option of leaving a small deposit and make the final purchase conditional upon the physical state of the dog when it is ready to leave the litter. The arrangement should include the return of your deposit if you don't like what you see at that time.

CO-OWNERSHIP:

In some cases, purebred registered dogs are co-owned. As the term implies, separate parties have an equal say regarding the breeding, showing and sale of a dog. Think of it as a business partnership with one asset - - the dog itself. This type of arrangement works great if the parties involved get along well, but if not, it can be the partnership from hell. Since these things often get fairly bloody in the long term, you should avoid any form of co-ownership, unless you are the best of friends. It would be wise to formulate a document with the terms of the partnership, including conditions under which it will be dissolved.

THE LEASE:

There is an equally awkward joint ownership arrangement called a Lease. Under this plan, the breeder is reluctant to transfer full or partial ownership of the puppy until certain contractual elements are agreed to and met. Failure of the buyer to comply will result in the return of the dog to the breeder. Sometimes this is avoided with a large, pre-agreed settlement upon closing. You are probably asking, "Why on earth, would anyone enter into such a deal?"

Here's how it usually works. The breeder sells a dog or dogs to you in return for the first pick of the first two subsequent breedings. In addition, he has exclusive rights to pick the stud and show the dog that he sold to you. You, in turn, get the right to have the dogs live with you, during which time you may train them and assume financial responsibility for any litters that are produced. At such time as all of the elements of the lease are satisfied, you become the sole owner of the dog. The problem here is that although you are housing the dogs, they are still owned by the breeder and a lease provides a temporary home for his pups. Good dogs get titled and poor dogs get fixed. You get the bill.

This sort of arrangement is much less subjective than co-ownership and does have a clearly defined time limit, however, I would caution the buyer to beware. There are some shady breeders out there offering some equally shady contracts to the unwary soul. Know what you are signing.

OLDER DOGS:

For some folks, the notion of raising a puppy is the hard route to dog ownership. My caution here is to be aware that you may be merely trading one set of tribulations for another. If you purchase an older dog, be ready for an animal with established habits and remember, he or she will still have to be adjusted to life in your home. Allowing for this, you have many preferable options available when purchasing an older dog.

As often happens in our modern, mobile economy, folks are forced to move rather suddenly and must find a new and suitable home for their dog. This is why, the walls of pet supply stores and veterinary offices are filled with advertisements for older dogs who are available. Remember those breeders who agreed to take back an unsatisfactory puppy sale? Well, they're also out in the marketplace trying to find a suitable home for a dog that is now a little older. Finally, there is no shortage of animal rescue leagues and humane society shelters.

There a lot of people in these rescue leagues and humane societies working hard to see that good dogs are placed with good families. They maintain clean facilities and see that the animals are properly immunized. Dogs are spayed or neutered when you pick them up for a nominal fee. You can get a lot of dog for very little money. In summary, I would investigate the older dog market in this order: local ads, Rescue Leagues, breeders and then the Humane Society. Why do I want to go to the Humane Society last? It is usually the last stop for most dogs. Using the other places first will prevent them from going through the Humane Society's doors at all. Believe me it helps. When I train a dog, I attempt to make a donation of money or materials to the non-profit groups I mentioned. We are all working together toward the same end.

LITTERMATES VS. BROTHER AND SISTER:

Littermates are pups whelped from the same litter. Brothers and sisters are pups whelped from the same parents but from different dates or breedings. Brothers and sisters can also be littermates. However, littermates can't be littermates if they were whelped from different litters with the same parents, but they are still brother and sister. Confused? Read it again.

MIXED BREED VS. PUREBRED:

There is nothing in the archives of wisdom that says mixed breeds cannot be excellent dogs. I have a mutt named *Mandy* who is an excellent housedog. One of the uncertainties of purchasing a mixed breed, however, is that you will probably not know what the puppy will look like when he grows up. Of course there are also some crossbreeds who are rather dense but the same is true for purebreds also. As far as training goes, I haven't had any problems with the ones I owned.

Look at it this way; throughout the evolution of dogdome, purebreds were often achieved by combining different purebreds in order to strengthen the stock. In order to get a modern mixed breed you must mix two separate purebreds. It's simple logic

UNREGISTERED PUREBRED:

Let us now consider the lowest form of dog royalty - the unregistered purebred. There is absolutely nothing wrong with this dog except there are no papers available to trace his ascension to the throne. I know a fellow who has some of the best hunting dogs that I have ever seen and they are all unregistered purebreds with no papers, yet they are all clinically purebreds.

Some breeders will sell you a dog without papers. In order to get papers; you have to pay them an extra fee. This makes no sense to me. The price of the dog should always include the cost of pedigree verification! If you want a dog without papers (unregistered purebred) then say so and the price might be reduced. Some breeder's also worry about selling a dog too close to his or her own market. This should not be a problem. If a breeder wishes to restrict the puppies breeding rights, then all he needs to do is check the restriction box on the papers.

**Zydie at one year. Here with owners Ryan and Amanda Wilson
Photo by Brenda Wilson**

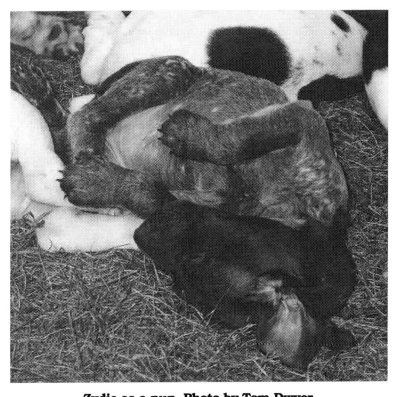

Zydie as a pup. Photo by Tom Dwyer

Be certain that you are comfortable with all of the other markings and colors. The dog will retain his hue for a very long time.

**Millbrook's Double Bogey with owner Fred Newcomb.
Photo by Pat Russell**

**Millbrook's Double Bogey
Photo by Pepron DiNatale**

The first thing to consider is the dog's disposition. You may observe this trait by watching the way that the new puppy socializes with his or her siblings. You will recognize this by the exclusive definition of their tails.

Millbrooks Whelping box. Starting from the left. We have Little Blue, Shadow, Sam, Heffernin, Zeek, Roxanne, Indi, Angel, Bob, Zydie (in the pile) and BB.
Photo by Tom Dwyer

Northerncross whelping box. Starting on the lower left. Northerncross' High Sierra, Sleeping Indian, Sage, Taste of the Chase, Bellamy, Blaze of Glory, Rosco, Silent Spring and finally, Brigadier. Photo by Kim Leeman

**This is Westminster Champion
Kates The Marqis O Jopavist,
Best of Breed September 1993.
We all know him as Axel.
Here with new owner Carol Horten.
Axel is adopted.**

New owner George Silva with breeder Tom Dwyer and Millbrooks Sassy Two-Tone.

CHAPTER III

BRINGING YOUR PUPPY HOME

This is usually a difficult time for the breeder. He says his good-byes, asks you to keep in touch, and to keep him informed on how the pup is doing. You assure him that you will let him know if you need his assistance. Although you are very excited, the puppy is definitely not.

AUTO CONFINEMENT:
    This is a very trying time for the little guy. He is being taken away from his littermates and dumped into brand new surroundings. Understand that it will take some time for him to get used to you, your family, other animals you may have, and his new living quarters. The ride home is a good place to start making him comfortable.

    The first order of business is to make sure that he is properly secured for the trip. A small box padded with a blanket, and placed in the bottom of the car will do very nicely. Better yet, place him in the box first then place the box into the car. If you can get hold of one, a small kennel traveler with a blanket will also do.

    Avoid the temptation to hold the puppy while the car is moving. He will have less chance of being injured if he is left alone. If, by some rare chance, he shows that he wants to be with you during the ride, go ahead and let him but the odds are that he will roll up in a ball and try to sleep.

MOTION SICKNESS:

It is entirely likely that your dog is going to become carsick. Like most animals, dogs are in control of their body balance when they are moving about on their own, but it's different when they are inside of a car. Their natural ability to maintain equilibrium is dramatically reduced. This is one of the reasons that they scramble about poking their heads out of the first open window they see. We all know what it's like to have motion sickness so, if you want to minimize the problem, be sure that he hasn't eaten prior to the ride. Now, aren't you glad that you weren't holding him? You would probably be sitting there with a fresh, pasty treat in your lap.

HOME AT LAST:

Once you arrive home, the pup will shortly have to piddle, so, get him out of the car and onto the ground. He will probably shake, sniff, and fuss around at first. Be patient and let him do his thing. When he is done, he will be ready to go inside. Recognize that he will be naturally reluctant so, let him explore the new surroundings at his own pace. Often by sitting on the floor, you will appear less intimidating to him. Also at this stage, there is little point calling him to you because you are just another part of his new and threatening environment. While he is wandering about looking for new things to sink his teeth into, just watch and perhaps try and come up with a name.

Be sure that there is food and water available for him. He probably won't eat much but he will most likely lap up most of the water. At this point, it would be wise to get him outside again. What? Too late you say? Well, it'll do no good to yell and throw things so, just clean it up.

For those of you who choose to keep the puppy in a kennel outside of the house, it is prudent to be sure that he has become adjusted to you and his new surroundings before leaving him outside. Most, but not all of the folks I know, will keep a new dog inside for a relatively short period of time until the new owner deems it necessary to put the dog out on a regular basis.

If all goes well, the puppy will soon become his usually cheerful self and start thinking in terms of a nap. This will happen after he finds what he feels is a nice, soft, cozy spot. Remember that spot as well as whatever he is sleeping on, for he will surely return there every time he wants to sleep in the future. So, why not simplify the process? Have an old blanket or coat without buttons ready and put it down for him to sleep on. When he wakes up, (and after he is put outside) move the blanket to where you want him to sleep. He will quickly associate the article and that spot with comfort. Now, he will be happy and you will have found a use for that old blanket.

Once the puppy has become acclimated be sure that you and other family members or friends handle him as much as possible; responsibly, of course. This will accomplish two things:

> 1. He will get used to being touched by others. This will help, down the road,

when he has to interact with trainers and veterinarians.

2. It will help the dog adjust socially within the home and around the neighborhood. Postal carriers and meter readers especially appreciate this. Like everyone else, they also enjoy being around a friendly dog.

YELLOW GRASS:

This is one of those inevitable situations when it comes to owning canines. Your lawn use to be the envy of the neighborhood but, unfortunately dogs also like the green carpet. On the other hand, your grass won't care for the arrangement.

Doggie urine has an extremely high acid content that will convert your lawn into lush green borders and punctuate it with an assortment of bald brown patches. There are some products on the market, including dog food, that are made to neutralize urine and waste. The bad news is that the urine will turn more alkaline, producing crystals in the urine. This will make it painful for your dog to urinate. His streams will become shorter, more frequent and he will soon be holding it for as long as possible for fear of the pain.

The choice is yours to make. You can either let your dog have the natural urine he was born with, or you can add the neutralizer, pamper your lawn, and have your dog pee in pain with crystallized urine: ouch!

CHOOSING A VETERINARIAN:

Now that Spot has settled in, it's time to shop for a veterinarian. Unless you already have one from a previous pet, choosing a vet could take a little time. I have two of them- that's right, two! One of them actually makes house calls. He is very helpful for nails, tails, and shots. In addition, he has lots of constructive ideas regarding raising and caring for my dogs. He is a personable fellow who often takes the time over a cup of coffee to discuss an issue or concern. He also has a low overhead. The second veterinarian is used for surgical procedures, heart worm testing, and emergency calls. I like him a lot also. I have come to know them both and trust them completely with my dogs.

It can be difficult for the first time dog owner to navigate through the world of veterinary medicine. Some vets will ask if they have treated your dog before and if not, they may tack on a "new dog fee" along with an emergency visit or examination fee. Be alert to this and ask about it before making a commitment.

Early one Saturday morning, one of my pups wandered away and was struck by a car. I called my vet to notify him before transporting the animal in my car. It turns out, he was out on another emergency, so, I called several other vets with the same bad luck. One of their answering services went so far as to call me back and tell me that the vet refused to return my call because I was not a regular client. So, there I was standing by the side of the road with an injured puppy, holding my neighbor's cell phone. My faith in the veterinary community was in the process of being trashed. Finally, I found an animal hospital in a nearby town who agreed to see the dog. What, I did not realize was that I represented a golden opportunity to substantially improve that hospital's cash flow. After examining the dog, *but before treating him*, I was told that the bill was going to be in excess of $1900. Please understand, I wasn't a regular customer. Since I was short of that fee by about $1300, I was left facing three painful options:

    A. Let the animal suffer for two or three days until my regular veterinarian was available.
    B. Incur a massive debt which I could not readily pay off.
    C. Put the animal down.

    I call this emergency gouging, a process void of any medical or business ethics. These people had an opportunistic shot at my checkbook and, since I could neither wait nor put the dog away, they were able to pick my pocket.

    This experience enabled me to develop two important theories concerning veterinary economics:

    1. Dogs will most likely get their shots on weekdays.
    2. Dogs will most likely get injured on weekends.

    It is also a good practice to visit any potential veterinary clinics whenever possible before making your final selection. Some clinics situated in or near busy strip malls usually have higher operating costs. They are also likely to utilize the services of other specialists. In many cases, they are not responsive to emergency calls and will probably only offer you the number of another clinic. If they object to your visiting them prior to being one of their clients, then you know precisely where they are parked relative to profit.

I prefer the veterinarian whose home and clinic are on the same property. They may be smaller but they are also more flexible and responsive to emergency situations. In the end, your animal will receive prompt, professional medical attention and that's really what it is all about. Understand that there are many fine veterinarians who will move heaven and earth to help your animal regardless of *where* their clinic is located. My observations in this area are fairly general and somewhat subjective; nevertheless, they have evolved from many years or experience as a breeder and trainer.

NEUTERING & SPAYING THE DOG:

Sooner or later, this issue crosses the mind of just about every dog owner. Although the question of whether or not to neuter a dog is up to you, the question of when to neuter is something you should discuss with your veterinarian. Personally, I know of three factors that influence the decision of whether or not to neuter.

1. Some vets live off the procedure....end of subject.
2. No more puppies.
3. Studies report that neutered dogs bite less. How much less is the question.

If you are purchasing a puppy with no intent of breeding him, then I would suggest having the dog fixed as soon as possible.

Schedule the procedure with your veterinarian. If, on the other hand, you are unsure about the possibility of breeding, then I suggest you delay the decision until about the age of two. This should give you enough time to see how the dog develops physically.

Delaying surgery can be a particular problem time in the case of spaying females. By the time she is two years old, she will have had four heat cycles and there's probably a lot of eligible bachelors wandering around your property -- leash laws or not. For the first time owner (if he is unsure about breeding) the first heat is usually enough of a crisis to send her to the vet.

A male is usually ready to breed at about 8 months while the females are ready at their first heat cycle which can occur any time between six months and two years of age. Even then, it is not etched in stone that she can be mated. So what does one do?

Personally, I would never submit a puppy to surgery before six months of age. Common sense dictates that he should be old enough to handle the surgery. In any case, why would you want to do it any earlier?

CHOCOLATE:

Over the years, many folks have told me that their dogs can eat chocolate without complications. These owners undoubtedly have never heard of theobromine which is related to caffeine and promotes seizures in canines. It can also effect the heart, kidneys, and central nervous system. Although different dogs react differently to theobromine, it is not good for any of them and even though the animal doesn't show an immediate reaction, it doesn't mean that you should allow him to continue eating chocolate. I would also make sure he avoids coffee, cocoa chips (landscaping chips), and the over fifty additional plants containing this chemical compound.

WORMS:

If you want good medical advice about worms, see your veterinarian. There are also many fine books on the subject which are well worth examining. The best I hope to do here is to give you some help with the warning signs.

All worms are dangerous to your dog. The worst, however, is the heartworm. The best way to combat this parasite is to have the dog tested once a year during his annual examination and supplement this with periodic worming medications.

Most dogs infected by the heartworm will tire quickly and, in a more advanced case, collapse entirely. Sometimes, they will also have a slight hacking cough. Any of these symptoms should send you off to the vet as soon as possible. Under no condition should you try to shortcut the problem by using medicine that was prescribed for another dog. Most medications are to *prevent* heartworm and will do little, if anything, for the animal who already has them. In other words, monthly heartworm treatments will not kill the adult worm. They are designed to eliminate these parasites before they reach adulthood.

Hookworms, whipworms, and roundworms, although not as serious a problem, should also be controlled by preventive measures. Taking a recent stool sample to the vet during the annual checkup is always advisable. If you don't worm your dog periodically, then there is a good chance that he or she will develop some kind of worm. If you notice that the dog is walking about rather gingerly or produces runny stools, then take your arm and place it under his abdomen and lift his hind quarters into the air. If this causes the dog to yip in pain then make an appointment with your vet.

HAIR LOSS & FLEAS

The same owners repeatedly approach me every year complaining their dog looses hair in the collar area and/or in the hindquarters. They claim that the hair loss occurs after constant scratching or biting, then the hair grows back after the next shedding.

The fact is that the dog most likely has fleas or a reaction to the fleabite. Every year the dog gets it and every year the owners go into denial. The reason why they don't see the little critters is because their dog is probably not the host. So, one more time, it's fleas!

MANGE:

Mites cause Demodex, Cheyletiella, or Scrcoptic mange. I would also point out that almost every dog has mites and that any increase in their population on the dog, in effect, advances the assault of mange. The mite's population increases when the dog's immune system weakens. The dog's immune system is what keeps the mites in check and although it has been argued that the strength of the immune system is a genetic trait, I am yet to be convinced that there is a gene/mite casual relationship.

It is also known that a dog can have a greater chance of contracting mange during different times of his life cycle, so under no circumstances should you have your dog neutered or spayed because of mange. Many articles have been written about mange and the mite, along with diagnosis and treatment, but I have also seen many contradictory articles that advocate castration. The cold, hard fact is that neutering your dog will not get rid of mange, nor will it prevent it from happening.

Most dogs usually fight off the spread of the mite infestation for as long as they live. Although mange can occur at any time, the dog's immune system seems to become more susceptible during certain periods in the dog's life. Since the immune system actually fights off the spread of the mite's population, fixing the dog simply doesn't fit into the equation. The proper course of action is to find out why your dog contracted mange in the first place. The immune system works less efficiently during the early stages of puppyhood, sick canines, and in very old dogs. Other factors which reduce the animals ability to fight off mites are puberty, certain foods, electronic fencing and chemicals.

Lets start with puberty. Most breeders will not breed their dogs until at least two years of age, but dogs really don't care about time lines and are not always inclined to wait for their reproductive organs to mature. The fact is, a male canine can breed at the ripe young age of eight months, which is coincidental with the occurrence of a bitch in her first heat. Hormonal changes usually start and end at around that age. This gives the mite a large window of opportunity.

Food should be your next concern. A good strong food base has always been the basic foundation for maintaining a dogs coat, however, food manufacturers are quick to sing praises about their additives. At this moment, I am looking at a bag of dog food. The front and back of the package states that it contains three omega fatty acids which is great for your dog's coat and aids in the regulation of his immune system. Often, however, our natural reaction to supermarket sales and coupons pushes us in the opposite direction. Arbitrary juggling of foods can compound your dog's dietary deficiencies and bring about intestinal irregularity as well as a week dull coat -- increasing the odds in favor of the mite.

The new problem in the neighborhood is electronic fencing. Lets say that the house next to you was just sold to a new neighbor that thinks his land extends to Mars and all the birds flying over his property actually belong to him. It follows that any other creature including your dog must fall into the same category. In this situation, electronic fencing can prove to be invaluable. It is an extremely efficient method of keeping your dog home without the use of a chain. Unfortunately, many dogs are being introduced to the fence at too early an age and at too high of an electrical charge. Electronic fences are beginning to take the place of basic family training. This is an unfortunate phenomenon but it has surfaced none the less.

Finally we come to the introduction of chemicals. The list of things that our animals absorb and ingest is long indeed: lawn fertilizers, dips, new and experimental vaccinations, ingestable flea pills, once a month wormers and heart worm pills (considered toxins), plant consumption (garden and household variety), floor cleaners, and shampoos. Obviously, we would never swallow this stuff ourselves; nonetheless, we unconsciously expose our animals to chemicals on a regular basis. The problem is complicated because when our dogs ingest those chemicals, the symptoms of mange are now camouflaged. In our rush to judgment, we think what we see as mange but in reality we are seeing the animals' reaction to the Sodium Bisulfate in the cleaner that we spilled on the floor. Even though it has been suggested that genetic traits may be one of the reasons for a weakened immune system, it is entirely possible that you and I contribute equally to the problem.

Mange has also been misdiagnosed as a flea allergy or other skin conditions so, get the facts before rushing into surgery. An actual genetic immune system deficiency will appear repeatedly and result in the dog undergoing a very long recovery period. So, *do* not fix your dog for mange, fix his defective immune system.

FOOD, COLLARS, & BEDDING:

At this point, a pet store should be of some value, provided you confine your shopping to supplies only. No looking in the window!

WHAT TO FEED YOUR DOG:

The breeder will probably give you enough food to last at least a couple days after you leave with his puppy. It's best to find out what he has been using because the transition is going to be difficult enough for the pup without his also having to make dietary adjustments. In addition, any food changes at this point might set his digestive system back a couple of days. This will likely manifest itself in the form of the runs. If you find for some reason that it is necessary to make a change, be sure that it is done with a top quality puppy food. Remember also that they burn a lot of energy. A quality grade kibble is all a healthy dog needs.

LAMB & RICE:

Lamb & rice is often the staple for sick dogs, older dogs that get an allergic reaction, or when the food is just not palatable. This type of diet helps stabilize their digestive system. The formula was derived from the time-tested recipe of hamburger and rice, which was traditionally fed to sick and ailing, dogs. Conversely, lamb & rice is not a staple for healthy dogs and pups. Anyone telling you that a certain brand of food is the best, has either a financial interest in the product, or simply has no clue about the digestive system of canines. All that dogs require is a good strong kibble with meat, chicken and fish being the primary ingredient. The food should contain adequate protein and sufficient moisture content. The food should also include vegetables and be enriched with omega-3 fatty acids.

Getting your dog off of lamb & rice will be very difficult. He will experience many problems such as vomiting and diarrhea, often for months on end, as his digestive system changes. It's like being locked into a high interest credit card when the limit peaks and you think it will never get paid off. Unless your dog needs to be on lamb and rice, it is best to get him off the stuff as soon as possible.

In order to accomplish this, take one large bag of lamb and rice and mix it with one large bag of chicken and rice. Feed your dog this mixture regularly until his stools return to normal. This could take anywhere from one to six months. Once he has stabilized, mix the chicken and rice with a regular food of your choice. Again, keep using this new mixture until his stools are normal, and then change over permanently to straight kibble. Both he and your wallet will be eternally grateful.

FAT DOGS:

There is a very simple solution to this growing problem and there are no barometers or weight ratios to go by. You know when your dog is fat. The first thing to do is fess-up and stop with the table scraps. The second is to cut his food to one half of what you would feed him on a daily basis. All you have to do is reduce the portions by fifty percent. For example, cut the four cups down to two. This will not fix the problem overnight, but it will slim your dog down in about four months, and make him more attentive. I guarantee it.

COLLARS:

You don't need one of these yet because your puppy is firmly ensconced in either the safety of your home or in his kennel. Besides, for the moment you can run faster than he can. It will be another three to eight weeks before you need a leash or a collar. When it comes time to buy a collar, get three different sizes because he will outgrow each of them within a few short weeks. Make the first one small and disposable and the second one a little stronger. The third should either be nylon or leather.

The clip-on collar was originally made as a breakaway collar. It is quick and easy to put on however, too much pressure can cause it to snap and break off. Adult dogs are better suited to wear the old "buckle" type collar. In the event that you have brought home an older dog, he should have come with a collar. The leash, along with its length and color are up to you.

CHEWY THINGS:

If you are like most new dog owners, you will probably lavish a variety of different chewy toys and rawhide bones on Fido. If you're lucky, he may settle upon one or two of them, and on rare occasions, pounce on the rest. It is far more likely that he will assume ownership of an item somewhere in the house that is better suited to his taste and chew on it for hours. Provided, of course, the item is not an antique, you might want to let him have it. Chances are, he will leave everything else in the house alone.

Rawhide and other chewable artifacts has always been an effective compliment to your dogs chewing needs, however, be careful of imported rawhide products. Some of them contain a preservative that in time could effect the internal organs of your dog.

At the other end of the cost spectrum, here are a couple of economic tips for toys that will vary according to the size of your puppy. To make the first toy, get a piece of rope, tie a couple of knots in it about two feet apart and then cut it at the end of the knots for a two foot play toy. He will probably go wild over it. For the second toy, put a tennis ball into a sock and tie off the end. He'll think it's his birthday.

Given the benefit of her own experiences, my wife suggests an additional caution: be sure and hide all stuffed animals or anything else that you deem sacred -- including the television remote and cell phone. Also, keep the coffee table clear at all times. Thank you Dear!

Which reminds me, be careful to make all articles around the home puppyproof in much the same manner that you would make them childproof. The only stipulations being that you increase the vertical safety boundary from three feet above the floor to five feet.

BEDDING:

Puppies really don't care if they live in the best house, ride in the finest car, or sleep in an imported bed. They understand sleeping on top of one another in a wooden box that was soft, cozy, warm and quiet. So, as I mentioned before, a bunch of old blankets or clothes without buttons will do just fine for now. Eventually, when you purchase his permanent bedding, you can be reasonably sure that he will sleep in it and not rip it up.

Some new owners even elect to let the puppy share a corner of the bed. If that's the case, be ready to get up whenever he gets up. Left to his own devices, the puppy will probably waddle over to the edge of the bed, give it a proper soaking and return to where he was sleeping. If it's any comfort, they tend not to pass stools where they sleep.

So, pick the place and make sure that it is cozy - but not pillowy cozy. If he feels safe there, he may well form a lifelong sleeping habit.

CEDAR:

    If you ever take your dog out hunting, jogging or hiking in the woods, I recommend crating your dog in a bed of cedar chips or shavings for the trip home. Not only is it the best bug deterrent on the market today, cedar is as natural as it gets. Coincidentally, in conjunction with the use of cedar chips, I would like to point out that there has never been a tick or flea infestation in my kennel.

Puppies understand sleeping on top of one another in a wooden box that was soft, cozy, warm and quiet. A bunch of old blankets or clothes without buttons will do just fine for now.

Millbrooks Tombe the Bombe with owner and
professional trainer Matt Doering.
Photo by Diane Doering

CHAPTER IV

TRAINERS

Most people elect to train their dog at home. This often works very nicely, in that they merely wish to train the animal so it adapts into their specific home environment. Once that has been accomplished, there is no need to go any further. Others choose to have their dogs trained outside of the home. Either they simply aren't capable, or the dog is difficult and requires professional help.

Most trainers agree that food rewards are the best way to get and hold your dog's attention during the early stages of training. Eventually, as the dog responds through conditioning, the food reward is eliminated.

To begin with, each command should be taught separately, thoroughly, and progressively. For example, the command "sit" must be taught alone until mastered. Only then will it be possible to progress to another command such as "down." Once "down" has been mastered, you may then combine the two commands and proceed to a third: and so on. This is necessary because some steps are harder for the dog to learn than others and you will have to use different techniques for each of the different commands.

Nothing however, will work unless the dog is focusing on you, so it is important that you remain flexible and adjust to his moods and temperament. For example, you might work for weeks on a particular command and think that you just about have it right when you suddenly give the dog a negative or inconsistent reaction only to discover that your bridge with him is gone and you are right back at square one. You'll recognize this the instant that it happens.

Lastly, there are as many different types of trainers as there are training techniques. They all basically start out using the same methods such as getting to know the dog. Sooner or later however, many trainers wander off into a variety of other methods, ranging from sheer dominance to clicker training. In the end, you can measure them by their results. On the next few pages, I will explain some of the training options available to you.

FINDING A GOOD TRAINER:

You've just spent a great deal of time finding the right dog for you and it makes sense to be just as methodical finding the right trainer for him. The best advice I can give to the new owner is, don't be afraid to ask questions and expect honest answers. You already have a fairly good idea of the level of performance which you expect from the dog and it follows that you expect to know with reasonable certainty that the trainer understands this and is capable of achieving the desired results. Your assessment of his sincerity is a pretty good barometer of the quality and stability of his proposed training program.

Give him my *at first sight* trainer test. When you drop off the dog, study the way that he greets the animal. I won't give you any standards by which to measure this encounter other than to note that if he lifts the puppy, tells you to come back in a month and shuts the door behind him; start to rethink your selection!

Finally, don't expect you're dog to be returned with the skill level of Rin Tin Tin. Most trainers will be fairly forthright and objective about this. Be prepared to accept the fact that your dog may have some limitations.

GROUP CLASSES:

This is the most popular and the least expensive training method. What's nice about group classes is that they are specifically designed to train the owner along with the dog. The classes usually last from six to eight weeks. They start with the trainer instructing the owners in the basics of simple canine commands and then the dog is taught how to respond to them. This type of course starts at the puppy level but intermediate sessions are also usually available. Certificates of Completion are awarded to the dog (and, by implication, to the owner) at the end of each class.

These classes do work. The key is to continue with the training long after the sessions are over. Unfortunately, many owners fail to follow up: consequently, the certificates get tossed into a drawer and Fido slowly begins to acquire new habits. "He used to do such wonderful things at the school," moans the owner, but he has forgotten that it was the *both* of them doing it at the school. The owner simply stopped doing his share. The more training is extended beyond the school, the better the dog's commands will remain fresh.

It's a fact of life that some dogs will learn better than others. Some owners feel they are not doing it right, while others think the dog is at fault. The major shortcoming with most group dog training classes is that they just come in vanilla.

Only one training format is used and little attention is paid to the individual animal's aptitude and ability; consequently, some dogs will progress faster than others. It may be that they are indeed smarter or that they more readily adapt to a particular technique. This further supports my position that one on one reinforcement should continue well beyond the life of the formal class.

INDIVIDUAL CLASSES:

As the name implies, this type of class consists of one owner, one trainer, and one dog. You pay a little more but the training methods are basically the same as those used in the larger groups. The advantage here is that better results will be achieved because the trainer's attention is focused on one dog only. Individual traits are identified and become the basis for a custom designed training regimen. As in the case of the larger classes, however, I must emphasize the importance of reinforcing the newly acquired disciplines well beyond the end of the program. Refresher courses are also available and quite often, trainers use these opportunities to work out any new problems that might have surfaced. Doggie daycare people will emphasize your canines need to socialize. But we, as people, want to teach dogs to socialize with humans. The local fire hydrant is not acceptable.

INDIVIDUAL CLASSES AT HOME:

This is a good example of getting what you pay for. Paraphrased slightly it means, *Big bucks bring big results*. Early on, during these sessions, you will probably just be a spectator: inasmuch as the trainer will spend the first few meetings playing with your dog. This will enable him to determine precisely what technique the dog would best respond to. As I noted before, the course will then be tailored to his needs.

For example, if he wants the dog to heel, he might work the animal into a "heel up" position, then turn the task over to you to follow up and reinforce. It's one thing for him to train the dog but his primary job is to educate the owner. In time, he will teach you how to react to most of your dog's motions and gestures. He will also encourage you to continue training the dog in his absence, because he knows that the best results will come when *you* work with the dog. So, don't excuse yourself from that daily workout. You're the one who will be living with the dog for a very long time. Remember, you're the customer and this trainer will probably be showing you every trick in his bag -- so, take full advantage of your time together.

KENNELED TRAINING:

In these instances, dogs are sent to kennels for individual training. They will be kenneled at the trainer's facility for several months and the training fee will usually include the dog's maintenance expenses. The trainer will probably advise you that it will take at least one month just to get to know your dog. This is not an exaggeration and the longer the dog is kept, the better the results. You can reasonably expect the finished product to be a finely tuned dog.

Unlike the individual classes at home, the trainer does all of the work and you will probably be unable to audit his efforts. On the other hand, he will show you his facilities and explain the techniques he is using in considerable detail. He will also be very frank and honest when appraising your dog's trainability. These trainers are usually top shelf, so be sure to get some recommendations or endorsements. You're paying for the very best and you're entitled to it. However, if he thinks the dog can't be trained according to his standards; he will not be taking the dog in.

When it's time to bring the dog home, expect it to be in at least, if not better than, the physical condition in which you left it. Take advantage of this conditioning and get him to strut his stuff on a regular basis. To do otherwise is a waste of the trainer's time, your money, and a fine animal.

SPECIALTY CLASSES:

I readily admit that there's a lot of stuff I learned as a young boy that has long been forgotten. This is probably because some of the knowledge I accumulated was never used. It is not surprising, therefore, that the same thing will happen to your highly trained dog. Some of his skills will become dormant from lack of use. When this happens, it is often time for a little fine-tuning. Towards the end, almost every club and organization in the continental United States offers specialty classes. It is a rare dog, however, who is considered perfect in both hunting and utility. Specialty classes are structured to focus on precisely that problem. In most dogs, this means one or two areas of performance.

These classes are not always geographically convenient, but there is another way around the problem. It is likely that your dog is not alone with his problem and that many other owners in your area are also looking for supplemental training support. If you're lucky, dog clubs or organizations might just offer specialized training for a given breed or class of dog. In these classes the trainers, owners and dogs all focus on a particular problem. These are great classes to go to and they usually result in a much better dog.

FINE TUNING:

The need for fine tuning usually surfaces when you attempt to work your dog after he has been inactive for a prolonged period of time. This happens more frequently with the hunting breeds because the hunting season is rather short and they don't get the opportunity to practice their skills on a regular basis. As luck usually has it, the summer flies by, and with the hunting season just around the corner, you simply don't have the time to invest in a protracted refresher course.

Should this happen, I suggest you either send the dog to your trainer or have the trainer make some visits to your home. Hopefully he will be the dog's original trainer - - if so, the training period will be much shorter. If this is not possible, allow for that 30 day "getting to know you" period, which we discussed earlier. A good dog has to stay sharp.

DOGGIE BOOT CAMP:

This is the mythical term that I use to describe the process of replacing the original basic training that your dog once had then lost. It also means that for one reason or another, Spot has gotten out of control and that you are going to have him intensively retrained as a last resort. Good for you and I applaud your patience, however, in too many of these cases, the wrong party is being sent to camp. I know, many owners think that it is the dog's fault but the larger question is *why was he permitted to deteriorate so badly in the first place?* Remember, good trainers strive hard to make the dog perform to the level which you expect. Equally as important, however, is the time and effort you spend expanding and reinforcing that training with your dog. The trainer merely got you out of the starting blocks. You and your dog now have to run the rest of the race by yourselves. Pay attention to the trainer's insights and training techniques and you will just about guarantee success. If this sounds redundant, it probably is.

SO, YOU WANT TO BE A TRAINER:

Everyone is good at something and this certainly applies to dog training. Expanding this truism, dog trainers are just regular folks who have both acquired the necessary teaching skills and learned how to apply them. In addition, the good ones continue to develop as trainers because of their genuine concern for the dogs and their inherent need to add to the body of training knowledge which already exists. If you see yourself in there somewhere, here are a few tips on how to acquire some of the more basic skills.

1. The first element of success is humility. Your way is not always the only way. You will meet a great many people whose only agenda is to share knowledge with you. This is because they are constantly learning new things themselves. Be appreciative, listen carefully, thank them, and sort out what you feel is important, and apply it whenever you can. There are no formal classes

required -- just a love of animals and a little patience.

It is also helpful to remember that the dog is going to have some lousy days just like the rest of us. As I pointed out in chapter one, some breeds of dogs are much harder to train than others; so, add a tablespoon full of patience to the mixture of humility and stir briskly.

2. I have touched repeatedly on the need to get to know the dog. This brings us to the element of patience. The dog wasn't born fully equipped to jump eagerly into the training process. Your task is to take the time to recognize his traits and quirks and utilize them to reinforce his learning experiences.

Let's say you have trained forty Labradors and are now working with number forty-one. He may be completely different than all of the others, or he may strongly resemble number six. If that's so, sort out what worked with number six and how you might apply that technique to number forty-one. On the other hand, also remember to avoid any mistakes that you may have made with number six.

3. If by chance, you happen to be training the animal for a fee, there is also the matter of integrity. There are two things that will probably surface as tests: first, the owner may expect something that the animal is not capable of: second, the owner feels that money is the principle element in your agreement. If either of these things surface early on, return the dog along with the money.

4. Be flexible. The dog and his new owner may have a domestic arrangement at home that could cause you to rewrite the training manual.

I once sold one of my dogs to a fellow who trained animals in Africa. "Tombe" was purchased because the owner always wanted to train his own hunting dog. The owner was confronted with the challenge of applying the skills of a domestic hunting dog to the wilds of the Dark Continent. This fellow fully realized that he would have to adjust his training methods and expectations in order to successfully train his new puppy. The last I heard, they were pretty much inseparable.

CHAPTER FIVE

DOMESTIC TRAINING

All dogs want to please their owners. They follow commands and perform tasks primarily for that reason; hence, a positive reaction from you will generally suffice as a reward -- along with a bowl of chow and a place to sleep. The best way to develop this relationship is to understand that proper training must parallel the growth of the puppy. For example, at the start, it will be necessary to use food treats along with simple hand motions and gestures in order to get the pup to respond to simple commands. As the puppy grows and matures, the food treats may be gradually eliminated and a more forced approach introduced. Forced training does not imply that the animal is harmed in any way, but rather commands are taught repeatedly until it is forced into the dogs memory. They then become reflexive habits. Once he reaches this level of performance, there will be no time delay between your command and his reaction.

It will soon become painfully obvious that you cannot train the dog unless he is focused upon the training task. For example, the most frustrating thing that happens to most new trainers is when they call the puppy to "come" and he just stands there happily wagging his tail. When this happens, he is not in open revolt; he simply has other priorities such as exploring a little more of the backyard. Don't fight it. He's on Mars and you're on Jupiter. Let him enjoy the moment. The worst possible thing that you can do is punish him for his lack of focus on you. No puppy will follow a first time command if he associates it with anger or pain. When he eventually gives in and comes to you, call him by name and praise him.

So, how do you get and keep his attention? Probably the best way is to remember that the puppy has a very short attention span. Just like any child, the attention of a puppy will wander more frequently than that of an older dog, so, keep the commands simple and the sessions short. They burn out quickly and need their naps. Remember also to keep an eye on his ears and tail. They are reliable indicators of whether or not he is listening to you.

DESTRUCTION BY PUPPIES:

We have touched on this briefly in one of the earlier chapters and there will be a great many things that you do not want your dog to do while in the house. We mentioned climbing on furniture and chewing table legs but those are just the tip of the iceberg. Whatever the offense, you are going to have to consistently monitor the problem. You make the ground rules and you enforce them. Chewing by pups is mostly due to the fact that they are teething while uncontrolled destructiveness is due to boredom. The latter will turn into a habit and, unless corrected, will eventually become part of his daily routine. When this happens, it is a time for firmness and reinforcement.

I have noticed that dams will discipline their puppies for various reasons as early as the weaning stage. For example, the bitch knows when it is time to start weaning her pups. She will growl harshly and bring her mouth to the back of the pup's neck. She will also use this method to make a point of dealing with other puppy issues. Likewise, when you grasp the back of a pups neck and tell him "no," he will recognize that he is being scolded. After a few times, the word "no" will be enough. Get into the habit of calling your dog to you after a disciplinary event. This will reinforce your accessibility to him at any and all times.

THE PIDDLE:

It's an unfortunate fact of puppy ownership that puppies are prone to irrigate certain areas of your home when least expected. So, let's discuss the *piddle.* The problem is compounded by the fact that a particular piddle often reinforces his need to piddle in that same spot forever and usually without warning. There are: nevertheless, some early movements such as the gyration of his body while smelling the ground that will tip you off when the event is about to happen. If you notice these movements, followed by a quick shift and a stop in reverse, followed by an arching of the tail, get him outside fast -- the other stuff is coming.

Like the rest of us, puppies are creatures of habit. Do you remember those newspapers lying all around the breeder's house when you first picked up the puppy? Your dog was conditioned to go on them during first few weeks of his life and his bladder isn't much stronger now than it was then. So, get those newspapers down and he will quickly remember why they are placed on the floor. Spread the newspapers in a spot on the floor that is easy to clean and avoid the obvious no-no places such as the new carpeting in your front room. Divorce courts are full of owners who forgot to do this.

Personally, I try to break them from the paper habit as quickly as possible. The trick is to change those random piddle events into more predictable ones. Like everyone else, your puppy can be trained to go at regular intervals; either on the paper or by going outside. The main problem with starting with paper is that it takes the dog much longer to learn to go outside because he is stuck with two problems: learn grass and unlearn paper. I recommend getting him to go outside as soon as possible.

Some piddles are clearly predictable. When your puppy first wakes up, carry him to the door and he will do his thing. About five minutes after he eats or drinks is another timely opportunity to familiarize him with the great outdoors. If he is being kept in a kennel cage, bring him outside immediately after removing him. Keep this up on a regular basis and you will soon find that he will start asking you for assistance. In time, he will begin to run to the door without your help. Be alert to his needs. If he doesn't make it in time, it might be because you wanted five more minutes to sleep. When this happens, consider it to be your fault.

Even if it is your fault, you will still have to scold him, so, be sure to do it right away. Yelling at him at the front door will discourage him from wanting him to go at that entrance. If you discipline him twenty minutes later, he won't have any idea why you are shouting and your face is so red. Dropping one in the middle of your bed is a good time to scold. Repetition is the key.

Work with the little fellow over and over again until he is conditioned and the piddle times are formed by habit. The ultimate habit being to piddle outside.

SOME WASTED ENERGY:

I have always wondered why so many owners teach their dog to beg by lifting his front paw. Is seems to be a rather undignified form of begging. Rolling over is another useless command. Outside of the circus effect, it does nothing functional to either the dog or you. You are going to have more than enough problems teaching your dog how to do the stuff that really matters, so why waste both his and your time with paws and rolls? I know many hunters who never even bothered to teach their dogs how to sit. They simply don't see the need for it.

"Come when called"
Emma with owner JoAnn Cardone
Photo by Tom Dwyer

COME WHEN CALLED:

This is usually a three step process:

1. The dog focuses on you.
2. The dog hears his name.
3. The dog comes to you.

Here's how it works. You will need some puppy treats. Something like a small piece of hotdog will work much better than his regular food. Place the treat in front of his nose and call his name: nothing else, just his name, then open your hand. Repeat this a couple of times and you will have his undivided attention. Now, take the treat over to the other side of the room, call the dog's name and place your hand near the ground. The dog will quickly associate his name with food and realize that in order to get that food, he must come to you. When he arrives, reward him with the treat, praise him for his good work, pat him a couple times, then let him go. Stop the training when you find that calling him for a treat simply results in the pup walking underfoot. Do it at random intervals and each time from a different distance, another room, or a different part of the house. You'll be surprised how quickly he will find you. Later on, you can attach words like "here" or "come" to his name. It will be much simpler to combine such words with the original command once he has learned it.

It is also a good idea to have one of these treats ready as a reward for his cooperation during a piddle crisis while outdoors. These small rewards can be used to call him back into the house and can be the beginning of your partnership with the dog. The food can be easily eliminated later on, but for now, he has begun to associate you with the reward. Remember, always greet or praise him when he completes a command even if he didn't perform to your satisfaction. He probably did his best and scolding should always be reserved for wrongdoing not for noncompliance.

"Come when called"
Merlin with owner Mike Luster
Photo by Tom Dwyer

"Look"
Millbrooks Independence owned by Cassandra Jorden
Photo by Anita Jorden

LOOK COMMAND:

The look command is a way to create *focus* between you and the dog. Say the word *look*, put a piece of cooked hamburger in your mouth and spit it towards his head. It's better to get him between the eyes. In time he will look at you with ears propped. Another way to do this is to have a whistle and another handful of food treats. While standing near the dog, blow the whistle once, while tossing a treat toward his head. If he is ignoring you, the treat will probably just bounce off his head but don't let that deter you. In no time, he will be turning toward you and catching the food. At some point you should delay tossing him the treat in order to see just how long you are able to hold his attention. Eventually, as in the two-whistle drill you should begin to withdraw the treat. In very short order, you will have been able to effectively incorporate single and double whistle blasts into his field commands.

KENNEL TRAINING:

Circumstances at home such as entertaining guests, dictate that, on occasion, the dog will have to be placed in a kennel somewhere else in the house. Training him to go into the kennel may not be as hard as you think. The first order of business is to place the kennel in a remote part of the house. If you keep it too close to where you are entertaining, he will probably yip and scratch because he wants to join in the festivities. Next, open the door, place a couple blankets inside of the kennel, and toss one of those reliable little food treats inside. Things will go much better if you use his regular bedding for blankets.

He will most likely go inside and retrieve the treat. Close and open the kennel door. Then he will probably exit the kennel, so, just walk away from him. After a short while, repeat the process and you will find that it will not be very hard to get his continued cooperation. Every once in a while, use the same hand motion but fake the toss. He will still go inside and look for it. Continue closing the door when he enters. Delay the amount of time it takes to open the kennel door. Finally, as you've done before, gradually withdraw the treat.

"Sit"
Emma with owner JoAnn Cardone
Photo by Tom Dwyer

SIT COMMAND:

How well you and your dog master the "sit" command is a good measure of just how well you will be doing with him on more complex commands. So, get your treat ready, call the puppy and show him the treat, but do not use the "sit" command. There's a 50/50 chance he might sit down right away and there's the same chance that he will start bouncing around trying to get the morsel. When he finally calms down and stands still, move the treat slowly over his head. He will follow it backwards until he leans far enough to force his backside into a sitting position. When this happens, give him the treat immediately. If, instead, he pulls away and gets up before you reward him, pull the treat away.

Without using the *sit* command, continue repeating the procedure and each time placing your hand over his head. You will have to get your own feel for just how long, but make it long enough that he doesn't become impatient and snap it from your hand. When the timing is right, let him gently take it from your hand. Once he has it, you may introduce the *sit* command. Thus begins his association of sitting with party time. In time, after a gradual withdrawal of the treats, you will able to implement this command with either a simple hand signal or by saying, "Sit." Smart dog, isn't he?

"Laying down"
Emma with owner JoAnn Cardone
Photo by Tom Dwyer

LAYING DOWN:

I don't know which is easier for the average puppy to learn: his name, or the *lay down* command. Both are fun to do, however, get your treat ready and make certain that the puppy has mastered the "Sit" command.

Once he has become focused on the morsel, let him watch as you place the food into your fist. Now, bring the fist down past his nose and onto the ground in front of him. As he leans toward it, he will slide forward from his sitting position onto the ground. Once he is properly down, open your fist and let him have his snack. If, however, he attempts to rise before the completion of the command, pull the treat away. As in the case of the other commands, you can start saying, d*own* after he gets the gist of what he is doing.

This is also a good time to start working on the *up* command. There is no need to say, "Up" or to use any treats. While the puppy is still in the *down* position, place your hand gently under his chest and smoothly whisk your hand back and forth. While you are doing this stroke him under his jaw with a slight lifting pressure. Move your hand over his head to give the sit gesture. He should move right back into a sitting position. Give him a treat! I know, I said no treats but, he's such a bright little guy and after all, he is sitting for you. Repeat the procedure.

"Stay"
Merlin with owner Mike Luster
Photo by Tom Dwyer

STAY:

At this point, you are going to test the dog's patience. Whether you teach the stay command to the dog while he is in the sit position or lying down is a personal choice. In either case, begin by moving slowly around him to see if he gets up to follow. Believe me, he will, and when he does, bring your hand up with the "Sit" gesture and make him sit down again. This time, have the palm of your hand slightly closer to his face: palm to nose. At this point, he will be waiting for a command. Continue to walk in front of him slowly and make him sit back down each time he gets up: palm to nose. Once he begins to remain seated, test to see how far away you can walk while he remains stationary: a few feet will do at first. Then, call him to come to you and repeat the procedure. He is now learning how to stay and as soon as he is comfortable with the command, you may incorporate the use of the word "stay."

This is probably a good time to start combining the commands: *come, sit, down*, and *up* during your work sessions. At first, continue food rewards for some commands while withdrawing them from others and see which ones he does best without food. The ones that he does poorly will require more work. That doesn't mean that you can neglect the commands that he responds to. They will still require reinforcement, after all he's just a puppy and he can forget things much faster than he learned them.

"Heeling"
Emma with owner JoAnn Cardone
Photo by Tom Dwyer

HEELING:

Once you have combined heeling with the rest of the domestic commands, the basic training will be complete. My experience has been that it is easier to *heel* older dogs than puppies. For that reason, I recommend teaching the *heel* command to older dogs before the *sit* and *down* commands. In the case of the older dog, proper heeling will enable him to better focus on you during subsequent lessons. In the puppy's case, he is simply not mature enough to handle it, and by waiting for him to grow a little, the command will more easily fall into place along with the other basic stuff he is learning.

It makes little difference to me whether you work the animal from the left or right side during this command. Do whatever you are comfortable with. This is only important if you are planning to show the dog. Suppose two handlers are walking their dogs down the same walkway going in different directions. If both handlers are heeling their dogs on the left, then the dogs will meet. This is not a good thing, so, once in a while I will heel a dog on the right. It avoids that sort of problem.

HEELING FOR PUPPIES:

You will need a puppy leash, making sure that the collar is slightly snug. You can check for the proper snugness by slipping three fingers between the collar and the dog's neck. With older dogs, place the collar more towards the head (the smallest part of the dog's neck) and use just two fingers to measure snugness. Placing the collar at the bottom of the neck on the older dog will only cause it to loosen as the collar pulls towards the top.

Hook your leash to his collar, remain stationary, and do not let the leash touch the ground. Think of the leash as a fishing rod -- when the puppy moves, so do you. Let him be the leader for a while as you gradually tighten up on the leash. When you want to stop, say "*halt*" and give a slight tug on the leash. He will be completely amazed that something is stopping him.

Next, call his name and start walking to the right or left. He's going to fight this for a while because he resents the new restraint. Encourage him to follow you using ever-so-slight jerks. At first, he will resist. He might even just stand there but, in time, he will learn to come on your signal. Whatever happens, never yank on the leash because he will simply roll over on his back and start chewing on it and you will have set the training session backward. Your primary concern, at this point, is to see that the leash is only used to guide his direction of movement. This is called <u>leash training</u>.

A twenty-five foot check cord may also be used to get and hold his attention. Hook one end to his collar and the other end to any stationary object: a tree will do nicely. Give him a little space to explore the immediate area and in no time flat, he will have gotten the check cord tangled in a bush or post. Guide him out of the mess and let him repeat the process. Soon, the puppy will recognize you as an ally and once you have his confidence, replace the cord with a leash and proceed with the task of heeling.

Puppies love to walk and this will give you an excellent opportunity to incorporate the *heel* command into his walking exercise. Training him to walk with you is no more difficult than it took to leash train him. With a slightly older puppy, you should also be able to incorporate the "heel up" command into the routine. When you want to walk him, simply tell him to "heel up" and then start walking. At first, it is best to keep a little distance between the two of you. When he wanders off to explore something of interest, repeat the "heel up" command, keep walking, and give a little tug on the leash. Similarly, any change of pace or direction should also be preceded by the same "heel up" warning. He will watch you to see where you are going and a little pressure on the leash will quickly bring him around. As he improves, you should draw him closer to you. All it takes is a little tug if he wanders too far away. Eventually, he will stay close to you, keeping an eye on your knees at all times.

This is also an excellent time to teach him the *halt* command. Simply say "halt" every time you stop. When you stop, make it a complete stop and be certain that the puppy does the same. Don't let him move very far from you once you have given the command and make sure that the leash is taut at that point. It has been my experience that dogs will learn to *halt* much sooner than they will learn to *heel*.

This chapter has focused on the basic techniques to be used for domestic training. The methodology that we have covered is time tested and almost universally applied. From time to time, new gadgetry or training concepts will pop up but upon close inspection, you will find that it is based upon the same common sense techniques that we have discussed here.

At the risk of being redundant, it is important that you get to know the dog before determining which training methodology will work best. Also remember that there is no clearly definable point in time when it is just right to discontinue training at one level of complexity and proceed to the next. Although I have pointed out the advisability to combining some commands such as *come, sit, down*, and *up*, there is no clear cut schedule for the typical owner to follow. I would presume, however to offer this general format for the order of the commands being taught as well as the use (or withdrawal) of food treats.

<u>First week</u>:	Call his name with food treats.
<u>Second week</u>:	1. Continue calling his name with food treats. 2. Start *Sit* command with food treats.
<u>Third week</u>:	1. Call his name without using food treats. 2. Include *Sit* word command with food treats. 3. Start *Down* command with food treats.
<u>Fourth Week</u>:	1. Say *Sit,* without food. 2. Start *Down* word command with food treats. 3. Begin leash training.

You get the idea. Keep the training timed and incremental and do not move the dog to the next level of training until he has accomplished all of the tricks within a given time frame, however you define it. There is no hard and fast rule that says all dogs will perform precisely the same and it is entirely possible, for example, that your dog might have to remain at level three for several weeks.

GENERAL HOUSEHOLD DEPORTMENT:

There is a better than even chance that the new addition to your household will find your couch a pleasant place to nap. There is an even better chance that he will take to teething on the legs of your brand new coffee table. If this behavior doesn't fit into your notion of proper domestic behavior, it should be stopped immediately. Some new owners mistakenly believe that six month old puppies are simply too young to benefit from discipline. The truth is that the longer you wait, the longer it will take to break his bad habits. Any means short of extreme physical force is fine. If the couch is fair game but the coffee table is off limits, let him know right away. It will save you both a lot of aggravation in the long run.

Come

Sit

Down

Stay

Heel

DOGS THAT JUMP ON YOU:

Dogs are social animals and as such, are always happy to see their masters. It is reasonable to expect that unless they are taught otherwise, you or your family may be in for some rough but innocent treatment. Unfortunately, many owners fail to discipline their animals when they do this, for fear of seeming too harsh. Not so! This is a dangerous habit that must be dealt with as soon as possible. When an adult dog jumps on you, raise your knee and press it firmly against his chest diaphragm. Apply enough pressure to show him that you mean business, and be ready for him to try it again and again. It may take a few pairs of soiled slacks before he gets the idea but he will eventually stop.

Like any other behavioral problems, this one is best corrected while he is still a puppy. In this case you simply do the same thing but with less force. Since he is a puppy, and you are going to have to bend over in order to get him off you, reach down and using the back of your wrist, apply pressure at the same spot near the diaphragm. Then simply push it up underneath him and force him away. This should be accompanied by a firm "no." Of course, no treats should be given.

COME WHEN CALLED FOR OLDER DOGS:

Although food techniques will most likely work, older dogs sometimes introduce a new challenge into the partnership equation. I have owned a couple of dogs that tested my patience. They would be fine outdoors for a short while and *boom*, suddenly they would scamper off into the woods or down the road. They would always come back, so I couldn't very well scold them. The problem was to prevent them from running away in the first place. I eventually solved the problem with an electric training collar.

I recommend the electric training collar with tongue in cheek. It works by inducing electric stimulation into the collar by remote control when the dog does something that he shouldn't. I use mine sparingly and judiciously -- never, never, for punishment. These collars should only be used when a dog already knows his commands and only after you have learned its proper use. You must also be sure that the collar is set at the correct setting and never handled by children.

First of all, the dog should be on a lead. The length of this lead will vary from dog to dog and leash to leash. Now call him. If he does not respond, call him again and energize the collar from the remote. He should move in your direction. If he does, be sure to praise him as he approaches you. You can also give him a piece of food if you like. If he turns away again, press the button until he stops. If he continues to ignore you while your finger is on the button, you probably have the collar set too low. Set it higher and repeat the procedure. Once he has been conditioned to immediate response, then remove the leash and try the collar with the dog at longer distances. Let him go as far as need be, but always keep him within sight.

"Come when called"
Jessie from the introduction with
Owner Marylou Kosmatka
Photos by Tom Dwyer

Do not overdue the use of the collar. If you do, the dog will simply become confused and stand without moving. You will have accomplished nothing and the training session will have regressed back to square one.

WHISTLE TRAINING:

The trainer who first incorporated the use of a whistle into his routine should be canonized. All too often when in the field, the owner will find his new dog chasing butterflies about 75 yards from where he should be. When this happens, I blow the whistle twice and see if the dog will come. He may or he may not. If not, I simply repeat the two whistles until he finally comes to where I am. Then, as mentioned earlier, I reward him with a food treat. Very quickly, he will learn to associate the two blasts on a whistle with a reward. As I mentioned in the piddle problem, you may then gradually withdraw the food treat. I always use whistle training first and reserve the electronic collar for only the more difficult dogs or for fine-tuning. Think about it. Why turn blue screaming his name when two trills of the whistle gets the job done.

"Sit"
Jessie with owner Marylou Kosmatka
Photo by Tom Dwyer

SIT COMMAND FOR OLDER DOGS:

Older dogs sometimes require a little more persuasion. In those cases, you will need a choke collar, a leash, and (if you have three hands) a treat. When placing the collar on the dog it is important that the collar be looped in the shape of a "p" with the leg of the "p" on the side of the dog that you are working from. If you fail to do this and loop it to form an inverted "d", the choker will not release properly.

While in a kneeling position, place one arm under the dog's rump while holding the leash in the other. Gently pull back on the leash and say, "sit." At the same time, move the other arm backwards under the rump to his hind legs. Be careful to adjust the tension on the choker to suit the speed at which he begins to sit down and remain kneeling once he is in a sitting position. Now, loosen the choker, pet him, and praise him for his fine work. If reaching under his rump doesn't appeal to you, then I would suggest pushing down on his rump while pulling on the leash. Both ways will work just fine.

Mastering this task will take the older dog somewhat longer than it will a puppy but once he gets the hang of it, you may dispense with the kneeling and stand facing him instead. From this position, bring your hand up over his head and pull on the leash while giving the *sit* command. Once he sits, ease up on the leash and pet him. Repeat the procedure until he begins to loose interest -- at which time it would be wise to end the session.

"Laying down"
Jessie with owner Marylou Kosmatka
Photos by Tom Dwyer

LAYING DOWN FOR OLDER DOGS:

With choker and leash in hand, let's now deal with your older dog. As you did with the puppy, make sure that he has properly learned his *sit* command so that he does not become confused and forgetful. If you find that he must relearn the *sit* command, then by all means, review the mechanics for sitting with him. Once that is done, manually explore the upper part of the dog's back and you will find a soft area between his shoulder blades and backbone. Place your thumb and index finger into this spot and while tugging slightly on the choker, press your fingers into his shoulder blades. It will not require much pressure to make him lay down, even less on the choker.

Once he is seated, stand up slowly. Now, while raising your hand, palm up, give a snappy voice command "Up", along with a quick jerk on the collar. If he doesn't move, place your foot under his chest, repeat the command, pull the chain and push your foot into his chest. He should rise. Repeat the procedure a few more times. Once he gets the hang of it, you may begin rewarding him with food treats. In no time, he will be responding quickly to your command. The more often you can get him to move consecutively down and up, the better he will retain the command.

"Stay"
Jessie with owner Marylou Kosmatka
Photos by Tom Dwyer

STAY FOR OLDER DOGS:

Simply use the same procedure that you did with the puppy, except that the dog must be on a lead with a choker. Have the palm of your hand closer to his face: palm to nose. Tighten the choker when he gets up and release it when he goes back down. Continue to walk in front of him slowly and make him sit back down each time he gets up: palm to nose. Once he begins to remain seated, test to see how far away you can walk while he remains stationary. You will have to be more patient with the older dog but this method usually works.

As you did with the puppy, combine the *come, sit, down*, and *up* commands and concentrate on the ones that need more work while continuing to reinforce the rest. Repetition is key here. Finally, remember that he is trying to please you, so, always end the sessions on a good note. A word or two of praise always helps.

"Heeling"
Rosa with owner Rita Spence
Photo by Tom Dwyer

HEELING FOR OLDER DOGS:

With the older dog, you will need to combine the use of both a choker and a leash. These sessions will be shorter and more direct but first, he has to recognize the two-foot rule. Stand completely still. Wait for your dog to move in a circle anywhere outside an imaginary two-foot radius. Jerk the leash when he does and repeat the procedure every time he moves. End the session after about ten minutes and repeat the training twice a day.

Next, while in the still position, you are going tell the dog to "heel up" by giving a slight tug on the leash, take two steps, saying "halt" then pulling back on the leash in order to stop him. Do not however, pull on the leash if he correctly responds to your command. You should end the session after ten minutes of training and repeat the session twice a day.

Now is a good time to tell the dog to *heel up* by giving a slight tug on the leash. Take a couple of steps, say *halt* in a firm voice and pull back on the leash. Repeat the process again using the *heel up* and *halt* commands accompanied by a tug on the leash where appropriate. Now try repeating the process after taking four steps. At this point, end the session and take up the process again a couple of hours later. Very soon, he will understand that *halt* means stop and *heel up* means go. Once this has been accomplished, you may begin taking longer walks with lots of turns. Remember, be certain to say *heel up* every time you alter your pace or direction. If the choker gets too tight, that means he is drifting too far from you. Pull him back and keep him within that two-foot radius. Start altering your turns: first wider, then sharper. You should even try an about face and see if he lets you pass before following in your direction.

To turn into the dog, you simply take your knee and walk into his head. His eyes will see your knee and will turn away. You might even catch his brow. Still, follow through with the leg. In conjunction with this, always give the dog an opportunity to catch up when you turn away from him. Remember, his task is to stay in the imaginary two-foot radius. His only basis for judgment are your knees, the choker, and the sound of your voice.

At this point, you will have learned a few things also. You will have calibrated your ability to apply the proper tension on the choker and you will have discovered how to manipulate the dog with less strenuous pulls on the leash. In no time, you will be pulling slightly, if not at all.

When the choker is hanging loose and the dogs eyes are on your knees, he will have completed the *heel* command. At this point, he will be much more receptive and you may now incorporate the *sit* command into the *heel* command.

One final note to all of this; heel the dog when *you* want to: not when *he* wants to. It insures his continued compliance and also reinforces your confidence.

This chapter has focused on the basic techniques to be used for domestic training. The methodology that we have covered is time tested and almost universally applied. From time to time, new gadgetry or training concepts will pop up but upon close inspection, you will find that it is based upon the same common sense techniques that we have discussed here.

Come when called

Sit

Down

Stay

Heal

SO THERE YOU HAVE IT:

Enough information to guide you through the necessary steps in locating, purchasing, caring, and training the dog of your choice. The manner, which these resources are allocated, is now in your hands.

The only other advice that I can offer, to ensure a safe and long-lived family relationship with your canine is as follows.

1. Watch your dog's food intake after puppyhood.
2. Vaccinate your dogs only when necessary.
3. Keep grooming up to date.
4. Bathe your dog when necessary.
5. Work with them as often as possible.
6. Never stress him to the point of fear.

Most things can be achieved in the simplest manner with the easiest solutions to the most common problems. Modern science along with solid old fashion values is the key to rearing quality dogs. I hope you enjoyed this book as much as I did putting it together.

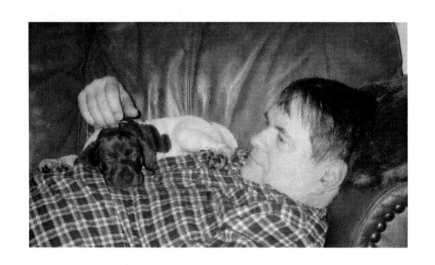

Enjoy Your Dog.

A Special Thanks to

Joann Cardone and Emma Lou

Matt Doering, Diane Doering and Tombe

Thomas F. Dwyer

Carol Horton and Axel

Cassandra Jordan and Indi

Marylou Kosmatka and Jessie

Kim Leeman and Northerncross Kennels

Mike Luster and Merlin

Fred Newcomb, Pat Russell and Birdland Kennels

Marianne L. Rousseau and Cedarbay Kennels

George Silva and Lucie

Rita Spence and Rosa

Ryan Wilson, Amanda Wilson and Zydie